Praise for
tether & lung

"Like the finest impressionist paintings, these poems' medium of linguistic light and shadow render the many nuances of a heartfelt and hard-won life, testament to the joys and sorrows of womanhood, motherhood, and marriage. Like the most arresting symphonies, the musical lyricism of these poems captivates the soul line by line. Like the most compelling collections, this book elucidates our understanding of struggles and hopes with utterly unique and surprising tropes."

—**RICHARD BLANCO**, fifth Presidential Inaugural Poet and author of *Homeland of my Body*

"With horse (gelding) as totem creature and knife (for the cutting of flowers and food) as totem object, *tether & lung* moves deftly and with sustained lyric intelligence through a bucolic world in breakdown. Here, the provisional Eden that marriage is, its daily soft violences, is laid bare for both husband and speaker—the husband tending horses during the day and surfing for gay porn at night while the speaker works the Catullan double-bind of hate and love, raising children, preparing food, marginalized and mistreated, but still with first longing. Lives, many lives, are at stake in these poems presented with an unresolved and mesmerizingly nuanced clarity that is human and true."

—**DENNIS HINRICHSEN**, author of *Dominion + Selected Poems*

"*tether & lung* treads through the liminal landscape of a relationship doomed. Pulled from dirt and Bible verse, this densely packed collection pieces out a disassemblage of bodies into grit, muck, and hoof. In the entropy we find the animal of desire as we twist through power struggles and the wicked beauty and violence of lives lived so closely with nature, tethered together by the fevered pitch of love, longing, and loss."

—**H. M. COTTON**, managing editor of
Birmingham Poetry Review

"Under the pressure of motherhood and her husband's sexual longing for men, Kimberly Ann Priest's speaker in *tether & lung* grapples with the needs of her own body. We witness her desire for her husband as she lingers on *the beam and bridge of his neck, shoulders and biceps rolling—sun-kissed dunes, a whole landscape,* all the while sensing he is unavailable to her touch. As a queer man, I find these poems deeply familiar—the steaming desire for what can't be returned, the journey through separation from other (which feels like separation from self), the acceptance that, even with healing, a part of us always feels *half-open, half-broken, half-withered, half-revived.* Sweet as jam trapped tight under lids of glass jars, each poem in *tether & lung* threatens an intimate explosion."

—**ROBERT CARR**, author of *The Heavy of Human Clouds*

"Priest's art is not for the timid, the faint. In *tether & lung*, she masterfully threads poems, one into another, widening the wound while expanding the heart. Each poem offers its own cadence, gathering momentum while moving through story, building song, containing pulse. Nature and human experience are braided together. *Tell me there are rivers, stars and trees*, says the speaker to her husband before she gives birth to their second child, all while believing, *mother-with-child is a lone animal clawing, coddling, carving home out of a wilderness.* Reading this book will force your heart to skip beats. Mostly, these poems will linger."

—**REBECCA EVANS**, author of *Tangled by Blood and Safe Handling*

*tether
& lung*

tether & lung

poems

Kimberly Ann Priest

TRP: The University Press of SHSU
Huntsville, Texas 77341

Copyright © 2025 Kimberly Ann Priest
All Rights Reserved

Library of Congress Cataloging-in-Publication Data

Names: Priest, Kimberly Ann, author.
Title: Tether & lung : poems / Kimberly Ann Priest.
Other titles: Tether and lung
Description: First edition. | Huntsville : TRP: The University Press of SHSU, [2025]
Identifiers: LCCN 2024018646 (print) | LCCN 2024018647 (ebook) | ISBN 9781680034066 (trade paperback) | ISBN 9781680034073 (ebook)
Subjects: LCSH: Rural gay men--Michigan--Poetry. | Gay men--Relations with heterosexual women--Poetry. | Gay men--Family relationships--Poetry. | Husbands--Sexual behavior--Poetry. | Closeted gay people--Family relationships--Poetry. | Family violence--Poetry. | Psychic trauma--Michigan--Poetry. | LCGFT: Poetry.
Classification: LCC PS3616.R5374 T48 2025 (print) | LCC PS3616.R5374 (ebook) | DDC 811/.6--dc23/eng/20240429
LC record available at https://lccn.loc.gov/2024018646
LC ebook record available at https://lccn.loc.gov/2024018647

FIRST EDITION

Cover photo and insert photo photographed by Kimberly Ann Priest
Cover photo and insert photo edited by Justin Hamm

Cover design by Cody Gates, Happenstance Type-O-Rama
Interior design by Maureen Forys, Happenstance Type-O-Rama

Printed and bound in the United States of America
First Edition Copyright: 2025

Gregory Orr, excerpt from "Horses" from *The Caged Owl: New and Selected Poems*. Copyright © 1980, 2002 by Gregory Orr. Reprinted with the permission of The Permissions Company, LLC on behalf of Copper Canyon Press, www.coppercanyonpress.org

TRP: The University Press of SHSU
Huntsville, Texas 77341
texasreviewpress.org

for Kory

[Contents]

The Gelding

My Husband Tells Me I Cannot Go Riding Again   3
Saturdays   5
Film Noir [with Car & Cigarette]   6
Weeding the Garden   8
The Knowledge Of   10
Homestead   12
The Good Wife   13
My Husband Tells Me He is Gay   15
A Study of Opiates   17
Into Another Country   18

Her Hand

Old-Fashioned Woman   23
The Chickens   24
After My Husband Tells Me He is Gay, My Body Contemplates
    Suicide   25
Flash Fiction [with Pét-Nat, Judy Garland & Bathrobe]   27
His Mouth   28
What's Left   29
A Needle is Found Protruding from a Bone   30
Self-Portrait [as Goldfinch in the Winter of
    Our Seventh Year]   32
Barn Burning   34
On Needing Someone to Be a Little Like God   35
We Dance   36

A Tether

His Fist   39

Nest   41

Through the Window   42

The Scrape   43

The Dead   44

A Tattoo is Inked Over Our Scars   46

A Most Harmless Hour   49

Cake   50

The Old Mare   51

Of Lungs

Gomorrah   55

Gaming   57

A Young Man is Beautiful   59

Divorce   60

Daughter as Still Life after Divorce [with Pear in Bowl in Kitchen]   61

Nostalgia for a Parasite   62

Up from the Woods   64

Poem [with Garden & Ghost & Issa]   66

Wanting You Back Again   68

Consider the Loquat   70

Notes   73

Acknowledgments   75

About the Author   77

Not Human   80

*it is her neck that sweats
beneath my hand, her sides
heaving between my thighs*

HORSES, GREGORY ORR

*And she said to him, 'Look,
I am standing in this darkness.'*

THE LOST BOOKS OF EDEN

the gelding

My Husband Tells Me I Cannot Go Riding Again

Swish of tail, stamp of hoof—the snow
pulled up against the barn for warmth

and the way the gelding nudges the ground
for any brush of grass,

his nose inhaling up,
broad teeth.

I tell you,
he knows I am the imposter

touching his side as though we are friends.
I want to saddle him up,

ride the field,
but this is not mine for the doing;

every animal has its own master.
He stamps

the ground to signal my insolence
roving one broad shoulder with my fingertips,

then twining them into his mane,
tempting power, asking

to be considered raw and wanting—
not chaste, not home again—but out there:

dirt in wind in tongue kicked up.
Like a mirror,

the gelding's eyes find me, glistening with cold.
In them, I see my husband moving

far across the way,
hanging the saddle he has oiled on its hook.

Saturdays

Sometimes we made pickles. Packed them tight,
poured brine, hot and salty—the kitchen soft with steam.

We cut each new batch by hand, knife sliced toward
the body, a clean half-cautious swipe. My husband

was quicker and crueler in all his calculations—
the edge of that blade like syllables severing soul-flesh leaving

tiny tugs of unseen grief. Ghosts are visible
on very rare occasions; the first time he waved the weapon

my direction, we were slicing pickles. He was careful
to keep the handle steady—quarter the fruit with its seeds.

Film Noir [with Car & Cigarette]

                            I tell him
to put the cigarettes away, don't exhale so close to my reaching.

Smoke in nostrils—   language.

           A gag of words that wick and saddle and chew,
           the driver's-side door creaking and plowed cornfields
                      rowing by.

My lungs seize up.

           He tells me to roll down the window.

           He says *fresh air.*
           He says *breathe.*

                            Smirk
                            & smile.

I don't say I want to be with him
coughing,
but cough anyway.

                            [asthma]

I am still *being* with him

wishing this was a *morning after* when he wanted me
   and the cigarette

  and I wanted him   again, after.

Frosty January cold fills my lungs.

     —I worship inhalation
      to make the silence natural.

Weeding the Garden

While weeding
the garden together,
I can do half
as much as you,
often trapping
the trowel beneath
a root,
unable to pull it out
so I let you do it
for me, and quietly
observe
your steady hand
working the handle
like a car jack
prying each thin wire
out of the earth,
a delicate extraction
of veins.
I lean over a pile
of roots,
as you carve into
the dirt
beside me
to dig up another
artery of weeds.
I fondle
loose filaments:
threadbare, tangled,
cut. You grope
at a thick sprout
of fuzzy
green leaves.

I comb. You heave.
Both of us doing
what we know
to do with weeds.

The Knowledge Of

> *It was evening, it was morning...*
> Genesis 1:31

Yesterday, we gardened side by side—he, a circle
pressed into the earth, me a seed.

Then washed dishes in the kitchen.
The June breeze balmy and ridiculously scented with loam

and bloom.
He hummed. I dried. Later,

he tinkered in the barn while I went searching for his wallet
wanting to know if my picture was still there,

dogeared, or if it had been replaced.
I have looked so many times past and always it is there

to make me question if anything is happening differently—
or if we are just in love this way. Differently.

At night, we listened for crickets outside the bedroom window
while counting each whinny and hoof

from horses in the pasture after going to bed early
but staying wide awake,

until he got up to smoke a cigarette without a word
and didn't return before I fell asleep,

so that I wondered how long he sat at the computer
in the living room before going outside to have another smoke.

His jawline always stiffened when he returned to kiss me
and I thought, perhaps, this was the way to kiss me.

Homestead

A copse of pine leans left opening the sky
as we round the bend of the barn, tattered remains
of a homestead

and I reach for his hand as he feels
the slanted wall of mangled gray boards with his other hand,
unholding my hand, letting it fall

consciously away. At home,
I like to watch him with the horses,
as he leads them with rope, sometimes with nothing—

the painted gelding following him around the barnyard
as though lost in the scent
of his freshly laundered shirt. Light angles

through the westward-facing window I hide behind
often, romancing the scene as it streams along his shoulders
and candles him till swallowed

by the full-leafed oaks that line the horizon.
This day, we lift our sandaled feet through the tall
uneven grass

and my husband squints into a sun
bound by rotations of time. I hook a finger into his pant
pocket, led through the field, up the hill, to the road.

The Good Wife

                    I find the place where you are locked under a rib
                          partly pried loose,

as if every part of you
is for opening.

                              You are landscape beneath:
spleen labeled fortunate, arteries depending, intestines inscribed
              borrowed from my father's first lies,

              all naked and pulling away from the bone.

              I want to look away but I am made to save you,
to wander among your origins,
configure the reasons you are portioned and exposed;

to scrape, suture, explain the scar that will inevitably show.

I use gauze and tape to set the rib,
        but feel it is not enough.

I apply too much aloe, burn too much incense,
        drink too much chamomile tea;

embrace too much of one religion
        and all the assistance I can muster
from self-help books and Ted Talks on shame.

I turn to the Internet and Google "how to set a rib without blame"

and discover it has been Googled a lot;

there is even a blog for this.

My Husband Tells Me He is Gay

The broken pipe beneath our kitchen sink pools
with rust and sweat

as his lean body bends into its twisted origami
like sculpture—modern art on display,

shiny aluminum tentacles tangled with manikin limbs
and torn up jeans, its Medusa

grown in all directions,
plastic heads smiling serendipitously at gawkers

as if self-assured, pleased with each synthetic affair
commencing where the upturned lips

meet inquiry.
Questions surface—bone and blood, gray matter,

the material of the heart.
He pounds a rhythm out of the sound his tools make

against the pipes
and into the worn paths between the tense muscles

of his abdomen.
My eyes dance like feral heathens along the beam

and bridge of his neck, shoulders
and biceps rolling—sun-kissed dunes, a whole landscape—

the fjord that dips between rib bones and thighs;
the rust and sweat

of all his aluminum parts wrestling, working, trying
to be a body in a room

where I am a lone curious stranger,
a tourist—the only other body his smile will greet.

A Study of Opiates

I remove my son's outer garments
to change him
for a good night's sleep

and watch his limbs gestate into
a uterine memory

that I remember too,
but not the same way.

In the womb, he would sooth himself
by placing his hands into his mouth
or on his penis;

the sensation he felt,
a sensation he needs.

He plays this seduction again in the crib—

how like a snake he appears,
coiling into himself.

Into Another Country

I must carry her through this, shove her straight ahead,
whisper love while feeling an undecided hate.
Why did I agree to this journey? Everyone watching,
like media mongers, to see if we will make it.

Some worry, wring their hands and pray.
Others gawk, entertained. And those not present
will examine our progress later with judgments and opinions
that I will hear when I'm most worn out.

A nurse fingers my vagina, describing the scene, telling me
how I should push with my next contraction.
I'll fucking show you how to push I think smiling warmly
into the ceiling, halogen lights dimmed for evening.

Tell me there are rivers, stars, and trees I say to my husband
pointing toward the window.

He has been here all along—little difference it makes because
mother-with-child is a lone animal clawing, coddling,
carving home out of a wilderness complete
with thighbone cups and dried leaf plates, snakeskin blankets,
rainwater drink, jack rabbit and aphid feast.

She and I were always one flesh and that's why, now
suddenly, as the rifting comes, and the wire jaws of Hell breech,
barbed and surging, our bodies rip from one another
and she breaks out into another country; then my body
retracts and breaks out too—

we inhabit our own bodies again, briefly,
until I grasp her in my arms here on the other side.

Wailing and tears—we are alive. *She* is alive.
Camera, lights.

Carloads of gaping bystanders ready to cradle her. They reach.
I reach. She is passed around the room.
Exhaustion overcomes my power to resist and retain her.
They have her. My body has me. She wails. I hear.

They will return her, I believe, held against my will by sleep.

her hand

❦

Old-Fashioned Woman

The suds in the bucket are soft between her fingers,
clouding up from the sponge

like pillows against the skin that will dry
and crack when she finishes if she fails

to lotion them enough.
Nothing feels as satisfying as the hours she wrings

water over linoleum floors
as though she is an old-fashioned woman

taking pride in the shine she leaves
everywhere, talking about her children

or a new recipe found on the Internet:
cinnamon scones that finally come out perfect

by the third and fourth batch.
She eats them every morning for three weeks, butter-less,

while the early silence reminds her
how long it's been since a phone call from family

or friends—a good book
set out on the table to enjoy an hour before

her daughter wakes up,
let's her mother hold her, feed her right out of her hand.

The Chickens

In the yard, the chickens peck mindlessly at broken shells
thrown out the back door
forgetting that these once held their own
unfertilized seed.

I watch them nibble at the calcite
and think about my womb—how hollow it feels—as a hen
rejects her tiniest offspring.

If God is Mother gathering her chicks beneath her wings,
why does the hen deny this little one refuge?

Everything in creation is soft and violent:

this morning, after sunrise, harvested eggs dashed to pieces
against my kitchen countertop
because my children are hungry.

With pangs I remember that I too must eat.

After My Husband Tells Me He is Gay, My Body Contemplates Suicide

The egg drops into a pot of boiling water, rocks—
stuck second hand on a clock. *Tock, tock,* it beats.

I coddle the embryo with my spoon for no other reason
than that I feel it might require touch

to communicate that the heat of this moment
is not about burning.

Bubbles fizz and surface from a crack in the shell
and I pretend that I can scoop them with a spoon.

Rocking becomes shaking as the egg is shocked
into denaturation

and proteins retreat from its walls,
clumping together like a little child curled in the corner

of a closet. Once
the water reaches boiling point, I withdraw my spoon,

put the top on the pan, look up at the clock,
keep track of the minutes

maneuvering distraction
out of the silverware in the drying rack

or from the stack of grocery store flyers
piled on the countertop.

Eight minutes and I assume the egg is solid in its shell.
I drop the ads to attend it

as though the seconds are imperative to survival
and remove the egg carefully from the pan,

I pat it dry, then spin it on the countertop to see
if it is hard enough inside—

the more tender the insides the more unstable the spin;
in fact, in its native state,

the egg would wobble so badly when spun
it might reel vicariously,

plunging its breakable body to the unforgivable surface
of the kitchen floor.

Flash Fiction [with Pét-Nat, Judy Garland & Bathrobe]

We danced once—
maybe it was twice.

Maybe,
there was candlelight, low light,

no light,
no music.

The sandpaper strength
of your jaw

against my forehead.
Slowness

and snow.
And the smell

of cologne.
Remember?

The ease of an evening
turning to morning,

sweat
on my pillow.

Sweat on my pillow;
I remember sometimes.

His Mouth

Together, our bodies displace shadows,
rocking back and forth beyond the moment
I hurt and he falls asleep.

My son's neck appears twisted as a hanged man
from an invisible rope
as he balances his head against my chest—

I am still learning the arc of his body,
how to keep it from following mine where the meat
is gaunt or the angle too sharp.

The moon wounds the mirror across the room
with its full expression.
We rock and rock and give it no rest—

past hunger and silence,
the call of a night owl and leaves rustling
the window where the wind is dusting off

our garden and preparing it for seed;
beyond morning when he bites me, scavenging
my nightshirt

for a few drops of milk, bruising my waking
with the apple of his mouth, laughing
as I wince from the pain.

What's Left

Imagine I am petting the soft head of a white peony,
full bloom, first cutting—holding it

in the hollowed-out crook of my arm, like an unbroken
egg, afraid of its yolk—the small chance

that it might leak inside the membrane,
and as soon as I open the shell, its once whole soul

will spill out onto the floor. And I,
in my hurried foolishness, quickly cleaning the mess,

rinsing it into a garbage disposal
until its last string of yellow goo is sucked

through the drain's black rubber teeth,
as I stand over it in horror, shell fragments littering

the countertop like torn petals, all that is left of you—
a sick reminder of me—

while the room grows wild with arms waiting to touch you,
and I want them to touch you,

take you far away from my negligence. It happens
so fast: the hospital gown, the heaving, all your shattered

pieces scattered in my lap, the bed begetting ghosts.
My hands screaming for what's left.

A Needle is Found Protruding from a Bone

I held your father when he asked the gods to punish him
for sewing a needle into his own flesh.

A fine seamstress he made embroidering his body
with textile tattoos, deepening scars

that would not show until the strings pulled out,
patterns vivid and intricate,

climbing torso and arms like a serpent threatening to twist
and tighten at his neck,

strong body holding his strong body—arms and legs
wrapping bone and tendon,

encircling, embracing,
squeezing hard and long until

pain became a word for *epiphany*, or just *another body*.
After which constriction

was not named *without breath*,
but *breathlessness*.

Many years and the bodies grew tired and loose.
Limbs fell, splayed, and re-rooted

as threads began to fray,
and the art of concealing lost its energy

so that the wounds in his flesh were visible, a pocked
and scaly apocalypse—

glaring invitation to what he had been expecting all along:
the gods presiding

internally, within bored holes and open veins,
evidence of iniquity.

And when the needle was discovered protruding from a bone,
revealing that the work of undoing

was the work of his own hands: *homosexual*—
the bodies he touched

not bodies to be touched,
not even his own molting flesh—he drew it out,

presented it to me. *Surely
a woman would understand this injury?*

Then got down on his knees for mercy;
he got down on his knees to keep from suffering alone.

Self-Portrait [as Goldfinch in the Winter of Our Seventh Year]

Such a small bandit now clutches the edge
of my bright copper pagoda

hanging from a large oak tree, assessing
the damages of winter;

my body behind a window. Time breaks
the hourglass, leaving streaks of white powder

that melt like old snow,
but the feeder intends to be permanent

as the goldfinch comes and goes
with his need, the wind.

In April, he will build a nest,
possessing its borders completely. In May,

he will be monogamous again,
a year passing through this miniature space.

A beakful of seed
tells me something about the way

we know our futures.
In any situation, real or imagined, always

desire—caloric.
I count my husband out each day

to determine how little I can adapt until
forgiving becomes forgetting to eat.

A lesson in shrinking;
the goldfinch, so small a body—barely enough.

Barn Burning

The moon dances staccato across the kitchen floor.
I wake at 4 AM and tiptoe
out of the bedroom for solitude at a window

framing the benign wilderness of ghostly stars, frost,
and anorexic trees. Last night,
you left the gelding out in the cold, ten-below,

after wrestling an hour to get him to enter the barn
then mumbling profanities from the field
to the back door of our trailer. Now,

shadows lick the snow a mere tongues-length
from a fire—the barn burning,
almost completely consumed—as the gelding kicks

and whinnies, tied to a fence nearby. I watch
from the window as you run, bare head and hands,
to work his tether loose then swat him into a gallop

away from the blaze. There is no saving the structure,
or rabbits and geese; they sizzle and squawk,
beat themselves senseless against the bolted doors.

On Needing Someone to Be a Little Like God

My son falls into the arms
of an overstuffed chair
and imitates his father
watching TV,
remote in hand, seduced
until he hears
the knob turn
on the trailer's backdoor
and lurches forward,
out of the chair,
bounding toward
the groan and clack
of hinges and feet,
trembling with facts
learned from cartoons
and fingers flavored
with crackers and cheese,
charging into
his father's open arms,
half a reflection of me
standing in the kitchen
with paring knife in hand,
seduced—
needing someone to be
a little like God
feeding, clothing, listening
as we try to understand
his absence from our day.

We Dance

My daughter and I use our bodies to tie the breeze
into ribbons—a landscape of swaying grasses, clover,
oak, and pine joining the dance. Even the berries
bob their heads on branchy necks, sparrows
catching them in pose, plucking shiny bodies, flying
away to feed their futures tucked into gutters
lining the roof of grandma and grandpa's house.
We spin around—her stuttering feet playing the earth
like a typewriter to keep up with her feral mind
where fiction whirls out of real life—the breeze
into a storm, the sun's limbs gathered
through clouds, the scent of secrets approaching,
grandma's laundry on a line behind the house pulling
at its seams—foxes, felines, and ferrets in nooks—
a forest and hunters treasure-laden with terrors and traps
jostling like a symphony of keys, each one
set and buried, camouflaged as roots or leaves.
A nest of tangled birch branches promising
an oracle of bugs that rollick beneath in the dark damp
dirt. But when it bites, it pulls a tongue pierced
through, one bloodied black ant kicking itself free
of saliva. All in vain. Ten legs strike the air,
the earth, the grave—*click, click*. Suddenly, my daughter
whoops loud and stops her twirling, falls down,
melts into the grass as grandpa teeters towards us
on one strong leg between two canes. We listen
to his laborious clap, clap—patient and frozen in place.
He smiles and shouts *Don't stop because of me!*
And we smile back until he turns to tend the bushes.
I melt into the grass beside my daughter. We dance.

a tether

His Fist

curled like
an unbloomed crocus
around a tiny bee—
tiny hate—
clinging to its center,
its wings
blaming God
for isolation—
Tongue tongue. Tongue
tongue.
It brushes
against his veins,
bruises.
Tired of licking—
dust in the lungs,
moist saffron.
He swallows
the bee;
I swallow
myself.
Both stick to the throat
of the crocus.
She pardons
the pain, blaming
us for misunderstanding;
holding her petals
like bridges
drawn,
refusing to open.
To breathe.
I panic
for breath.
He curls his earlobes,

pants.
Burns an army of wings
behind him,
loves
the dance.
Enters the crocus
through a petal's charred
remains,
begins buzzing—does
everything he can
to stop.

Nest

Manure scented grass girds the breeze slipping through
a slit of window, a mere two inches that I open
to breathe my first bit of fresh air since October last year.

Everything is changing: the house a pair of lungs,
field mice running away and new sparrows in the awning.
All the doors shifting in their sills.

My husband's muddy boots thawing in a puddle on the porch
near a bench swing. *Not yet* it sighs into its ceiling hooks
and chains. It's still ten degrees too cool to be outdoors

so I pull my sweater tighter, inviting the chill
through the window, as sunlight warms a spot on the couch
large enough to coddle my body—my husband's body

small enough to also fit into its space. Alone, I hold
our two bodies, tuck my fingers beneath my thighs, build
a nest in some plausible corner of my mind.

Through the Window

The boy shadows her, his five-foot-seven frame
several inches taller,

and his shoulders, wider—even
his smile grows larger than hers on his face. She is

womanly, and not. She is
powerful

and not.
She grew quickly into her withers and mane

until she became
one of her father's horses

owning the barnyard so completely
they don't even need to make the ground quake.

But they do,
sometimes.

Through the window I watch them accelerate,
pound the field,

shimmy with adolescence.
Like my daughter with her headphones on: shake, shake,

shake—free as she can be
in a bathrobe before she gives a damn about

her hair, her hips,
her face.

The Scrape

You split sunset with your lean silhouette. I see you
as I need to—godly, in a Carhart jacket and torn up jeans,
watching the horses stop and break into gallops
and kicks, leaving pockmarks all over the pasture,
the fences holding them in and cutting your body
in three at torso and knees, your elbows curled backward
over the top rung, back straight. And I want to feel
a small pang of pity or sadness to say I am a little
comforted by your pain, a little less angry because
you are hurting, a little understanding because I am hurting
too from the awful scream you tore through me
after dinner in the bedroom, the children's ears barely
out of reach. I want to say it must be heavy to carry
such a secret, to feel your body roving with an unrepentant
shame. To be gay and married to me and able to tell
no one of importance, your family dedicated to
a Christian faith. I watch you through the window
hoping you will not return but stay there with the horses
or run off to be with a man of your choice, not because
I am kind this way or want you happy, but because
you've named me, again, the things you feel are you:
adulterer, liar, insane. You shift your weight
into the fence post, elbow slips. I lift my hand in a motion
to catch it, wincing as you coddle the scrape.

The Dead

We peel our bodies
from the inside
of bodies,

tiny we are, not
tiny again—

each time we peel, we are

bodies
coming out
of these bodies.

Are membrane in shell, or
outside of shell.

Are rocked animal in arms,
reproducer and produced.

Part of me is seeking
asylum,
the other part searching
for food.

Reach for me beneath
the covers tonight,
Lover.
Wrap me thinly in your arms,
the start

of yet another question:
am I consumer
or consumed?

Am I keeping
your spirit
from lifting?

Or giving you reason
never
to move?

A Tattoo is Inked Over Our Scars

> .... *and the amaranth said to her neighbor, "How I envy your beauty and your sweet scent...."*
> *Aesop*

      Where our shoulders kiss: a soft coloring of pink spreading, blooming side by side—a single stalk.

Petals bleed over our chests, across our backs—ivory, white, deeper shades of fuchsia:

                  we are drunk with memory, reeling, I hold
                        you steady with unsteady hands,

              as we draw circles around the bruise
                    of lung and spleen,

            of living body.

Do not name this sorrow, I say, *name this unfading instead.*

In paradise,
we will call it

           Gethsemane, the place
              of ears, the blood
           of martyrs streaming down our necks.

I tell you not to touch it—let it bleed across your jawline
from where we share a mutual scar. Let

the artist do his work, needle
organs into place, whisper fortune—tell the one but not the other
where these energies will lead once escorted from this place.

                    You purchase
          silence and another pack of cigarettes.

Smoke.

The amaranth grows wildly inside us, burrowing its root
      into our limbs,
feeding as it does on our complying—and we have been here

long enough to know to breathe first last.

Forget the sound our petals make when they ready themselves
    for dying,

the garden growing with parasite. The final time you will look
    at a woman and see God. And God

will see and call this *good*, this thing you do with your body,

        your left hand holding an ear, a startled pain,
        a knife—not mine

    clatters to the kitchen floor.

        You point in my direction
        moaning.

    Our vanities flower and break.

A Most Harmless Hour

The men are out working the fields, rolling hay into tight spirals,
then leaving them to harvest another day.

They dot the landscape like butterscotch pinwheels
I trace on the window with my finger

before walking outside to ornament my eyes
with the picturesque view.

The tractor slows into its cave under an awning. You dismount,
wiping your forehead against the sweaty bare skin

of your arm. A smearing, a full bottle of water
drunk down, your body all heat.

Labor's satisfaction starving the parts of you more animal—
less philosophic inquiry or need to muse over

an injury. The god-sent sweet exhaustion
that overcomes a soul when all its muscles have been used.

This is a most harmless hour—the tractor holding your ribcage
like a man steadying a woman worn from giving birth.

Cake

In the morning, when sunlight slices our bed
into single servings of cake—lines repeated
through the window shade—and you wrestle
with waking dreams, your mouth mouthing
what I hope will one day turn out to be
my name (*naming* sometimes being an act
of *loving*), and the blood rushes
into my eardrums, a tingly sensation in my lips,
just like the first time I saw you at a party
and, without thinking, reached to brush crumbs
off of your shirt, then stopped myself—my
touch being so much more than maintenance,
but maintenance all the same, yet meaning
I want you to touch me this way, the way
animals groom each other in public as though
no one is looking—even the private parts.
They nibble and devour. Nature not being
as socialized as we are when not holding,
or kissing here but not there. In our bed, nervous
dashes of light dance at the back of your neck
and I want to spin them with my tongue.
I would too, but you have taught me the way
and the way not to wake you. So these are the hours
I want you before you know I want you
to touch me, this woman, like you wanted
the dark-skinned man at the party. I saw you
eye him with your fork in hand, fondling
desire on a plate, things done not *here* but *there*,
things mouthed across a room, a secret,
a name, a private longing moving slowly
over your body in my bed, devouring your lips.

The Old Mare

She stands close to the barn, its angle
guarding her from a northerly wind—a storm approaching;
while the painted gelding prances in the arena,
then kicks into full stride.

He embraces the power inherent in the hours between
the inevitable and its arrival.
Something about danger, something about
taunting its path. Something unlike the letter I wrote

and left on your pillow last night before I went
to bed: *Tried to call. Not sure where you are. Hope you are
safe.* And, in the morning, it was gone—
you were already out with the horses securing the scene,

a bluster of winter stirring at your heels. Here,
the weather changes so swiftly and the old mare has learned
what the gelding has not: conserve
your energy—its heat could keep you alive this night.

*of
lungs*

Gomorrah

There are dead things—*bright dead things* says the poet
Ada Limón—in my flower sink.

Plant scraps, like leftover paper after cutting something out—
green pieces dead, but not dead yet,

sitting at the bottom of my sink, weighted.
My murderous hands caressing each stem and leaf

as I repent to myself *I'm so sorry, I had to chop you off.*
There was no proof of anything. No incrimination. No criminal.

Only indifference to my supple back and breasts.
Only the flowers you brought home as expected. Only that

sometimes you were not at work when I called
though you told me you would be.

The bed sheets still smell of your sweat,
the scent steaming after I shower and roll my body around

underneath the covers to feel all of the space.
I am glad your sweat has not washed out; as I am glad you are

no longer in my bed. Once,
you nearly used a handful of my hair to move me in sleep,

but stopped yourself.
Many times, I touched your hair while you slept to satisfy my grief.

I hold my scissors over the sink and prune a few more stems
from the lower layers of this philodendron—

strong totems spearing upward from its leafy bush,
leaves dropped around its terra cotta base as though in ceremony,

like the dark warm pain that smoldered and danced around
my empty city till it tombed

when I saw the tiny box imbedded on our computer—two tangled
naked miniature men, bodies tightly wound

in a casket-size embrace;
the sex of it so foreign to my limbs, I lingered, and clicked.

Gaming

for my son

Blinking dots in a bruised landscape,
        bodies shattered
in sudden explosion,

the small keypad that dips and drums
        beneath your fingers
leading your alter ego

through a manufactured war—guns
        and dragons,
combat women, beautiful swords.

Your father mocks this mission
        of arched back
and concentrating eyes because

at your age, he says,
        he was outside in the barn
tending horses,

late into the night oiling the saddles,
        filling buckets with grain, digging
rocks out of his painted gelding's

shoes. Constructive in his meditative
        practice—becoming
a man alone.

The gelding still holds all of your father's
        secrets in one-sided
private exchange—

so different from the conversation you make
        with your friend
over the mic attached

to your headphones. Together
        you slay at least one hundred
giants, build tanks, blow up limbs,

burn down cities, turn off the game
        and strategize the next.
Hours wasted in laughter, dirty jokes,

and surprise—what you can do to entertain
        a friend who is autistic
and often isolated

in a house down the street from your own
        where he sits on his bed
with headphones on, a mic, a small keypad,

and whelps loud after beating his enemy, you
        shaking your head and smiling
happy to be the loser again.

A Young Man is Beautiful

Sunrise behind a curtain: thin fortress against
the over-bright dawn where he,

beneath the bedroom window,
plucks dry petals from the first signs of spring.

I collapse into our bed sheets
unready for this day, finding him

in the scent of daffodil coming through
the screen. Last night,

I stayed outside too long listening to frogs
chorus the stars while he slept

by the glow of a nightlight caressing
the side of his face. Late,

I stood in our bedroom doorframe
enacting a private exploration of his features

like a schoolgirl seeing a young man is beautiful
for the very first time. He was

beautiful, stirring as I laid down beside him
and murmuring something against

the side of his face. In a dream state,
he reached for me playfully

then turned away—the closed center of a bud
unfurling, shaking his dead stuff away.

Divorce

My husband had honey-colored eyes and honey-colored hair
and he broke his teeth into the flesh of a strawberry
as though it were something to jump rope with, never a bleed
of juice left on his lips.

His shoulders were shrined in cotton year-round,
taut to the bone with summer rituals of baling hay, and in winter
the rigor of shovels or pulling our children in sleds.

He could bounce a smile off an egg freshly dropped
from our chickens in the barn behind the house where he spent hours
adapting the rhythm of a pitchfork to his tenor—

its strong, sonorous vibrato rising over the grunts of his horses,
all of which he nuzzled daily, kissed, and called by name,

commanding them to lift their legs, inspecting their hooves,
digging mud and rock out of their shoes; and they did with ease,
because they knew he loved them.

He would, with equal care, tighten the lids on every jar of jam
we canned together with berries we had picked together,
cleaned, then cooked. And after a long day of barn work and jars
cooling on towels in the kitchen, he'd wash the sweat off of his body
in the shower, careful to turn on the overhead fan to keep
the bathroom from filling with steam.

That night, I would lie next to him in bed and, with my eyes,
rove the stubble on his jaw, under his chin, down the steeple
of his neck, answer the shallow of his breath with my questions.

**Daughter as Still Life after Divorce
[with Pear in Bowl in Kitchen]**

a contrapuntal

Seed socket—this you call my nucleus, infant belly
dropped and petrified.

Something I can't chew will be
all that is left of me.   I ripen

like a window
turns yellow
with too much daylight,
slicking my dark shaft white,   you think.

Mother can't oil me to core. I am not
that open,
my pistons don't move: up and down, my

how sweet you look trying
to generate a shadow
as you turn me toward the sun.   My
how sweet you look Mother,   like something
                                           I could bite.

Nostalgia for a Parasite

If I forget your name, let the aphids drink
my amber dreams,

let them get drunk on the wine of my body, let them
warp and ripple the leaves

until they drop—my worn t-shirt and torn jeans
heaped in a pile on the floor

as I curl into a temporary craving
for you,

yet gather nothing but myself into my hand
and feel the ache and sweat of my

own energies that secrete their poisons
for no purpose outside of their

own purpose. Let me search endlessly for someone
in the countryside, the city,

the crowds, the corridors, the streets
to be an anti-parasite

kissing all over my body, ingesting my dark longing
for your body,

each press of flesh forgiving me for what
I do not have to offer

any other man: a bloom, a sturdy stem, unfurled
leaves, a bath

of water in a vase perfectly arranged, a card
with an inscription and a name.

Up from the Woods

A twelve-year old boy pulls a pocketknife out of his pocket
and fidgets with it, unopened, spins it in the palm of his hand
to animate the kill. One bullet—the first he'd ever shot
from a rifle—hit the small buck in the jugular taking him down
swiftly. My son is a hunter now, his grandfather
hitching up the trailer to retrieve the body out of the woods.

He can barely solicit my son's attention as my son tells me the story
for the third and fourth time: Grandpa never saw the deer,
but I spotted it out of the corner of my eye and reached
for the gun, tugged at grandpa's pant leg pointing with my head
in the direction of the buck. *Grandpa gives me the rifle and bang!
The buck drops into the snow. One shot. Me and grandpa*

*climb down to the deer to inspect it, make sure it's dead.
Then grandpa pulls out his large hunting knife and slices the throat,
lets the stag's blood run out all over the ground* . . . Later
that evening my son refuses to gut the deer in the barn, prepare it
for food. Instead, he tells me the tale of the *one shot* over and over
again, as I sit by the light of his storytelling eyes to learn the art

of intonation and silence, nuance describing itself in the pauses
between his short breaths—wind in trees—all the light in the room
shifting shadows through leaves, his lips reenacting the pitch
of a whippoorwill's call, and his arms, a hawk encircling prey,
how the ruffed grouse beats its wings rapidly against the ground
in a *thrump-thrump-thrump* that can be heard miles through the forest

drumming for its mate—the fact that some birds survive here
through winter, and rabbits foraging leftover berries and green, snow

turning purple beneath a cloudy sky, endangering footprints
up from the woods, the subtle scent of pinesap between our fingers,
difficult to clean off even with gasoline—laughter. We consume
a whole bowl of popcorn. He tells me he will never go hunting again.

Poem [with Garden & Ghost & Issa]

                                          I am trying to repent—

of the subtle language of kisses,
how his lips parted only just

so, enough;

                    and honor the crossing of our bridges

                    with sackcloth and ashes.

For seeing him differently

                —clean & beautiful
                & holding himself too rigid,

                too much in place,

                    so that his hands—stiff inside his pockets—needed
                            an offering, a folding.

[Posing.]

        Our children

        evaporate like dreams

as all my tears come late—   & he summons himself
           like a ghost
           into an afterlife
           with his second Adam

     until, says Issa, *all our world* [is] *dew.*

Because,

every man is seed,
even the homosexual ones.

[For this,   I am trying to repent].

Wanting You Back Again

I cut your eyelids out of the saucepan, reduce the heat,
increase the salt.

My mother sent a card to say she is sorry you were
unkind to me.

The digital clock calculates the number of times
the spoon rolls butter off its tongue
into wax dots of maple candy bargaining
for more portraits of *home,* what children should feel
November mornings when the leaves turn burnt honey,
and the silos grow silent with corn dust and grain.

Is it betrayal to say I loved my life with you?

Sweat on the screen door in summer,
pine and lemon oil pressed into my palm feeling a damp cloth
over the curved legs of a table, Sinatra on CD
combing tenor through the rustling oak in our backyard,
our children running laps beneath its open chest,
my puppy pawing at my leg, three potted herb plants
waking on a sill.

All of this while you were not at home.

We saw your sister's new baby, the card reads.
I press my thumbprint into one shiny blob of cooling sap—
the wanting that comes with waiting for something
to take shape, give itself over to the lips;

anything to remember your footsteps at the backdoor
never came with the same anticipation that one has
for autumn, because it *feels* like apples.

A thin layer of syrup thickens at the bottom
of the saucepan,
clock digits explaining only six minutes have passed—
my daughter's hand stabbing at the cushion of your chair
at an angle I can see.

Consider the Loquat

for my daughter

I pack your liver into my suitcase
since I would not feel generous or poetic
stealing away your heart

and since *liver* means the same as *heart*
in ancient poetry,
and I imagine this is because

like them I feel this pain
in my gut, not my chest, as though
the wind has been knocked out of me

so hard I'm not sure I am doing
the thing I am doing—
leaving you.

I'm not sure I can see it this way,
not now; rather,
I must pretend that we are doing something

different. Perhaps, going on extended
separate journeys. Or, submitting ourselves
to some divinely ordained plan.

Maybe we are a river
breaking in its path to form two independent
streams,

or we are like the loquat tree
that blooms out of season
and I should not think about this whole thing

too much, about
how it might be unnatural to leave you
at fifteen, barely a woman,

assuring me that now is a good time
to go—as though the deep reds
and yellows of autumn are a sign,

a portent,
and I would be a fool if I did not heed
the warning in your eyes. You know me

too well, my daughter. You know
I will feel this pain long enough to wish
I had stolen your heart.

Notes

The epigraph for "The Knowledge Of" comes from the creation myth in Genesis, the Bible.

"A Study of Opiates" refers to theories on social attachment in which the endogenous opiates system is understood as primarily responsible for maintenance of "dyadic social and maternal/infant pairbonds" in "nonhuman primates." According to A. J. Machin and R. I. M Dunbar in "The brain opioid theory of social attachment: a review of evidence," there is also "direct experiential evidence" among humans "suggesting that involvement in a romantic or supportive relationship explicitly elevates pain thresholds, suggesting that endorphin titres may be higher during active relationships." And that "[....] endogenous opioids may play the maintenance role which is vital for, among other things, stable long-term relationships and the rearing of psychologically healthy, socially adept human beings." [source: *Behaviour*, Vol. 148, No. 9/10 (2011), pp. 985-1025]

"Into Another Country" was partly inspired by increased anxieties and renewed conflicts concerning immigration at the Mexican border. "Border crossers and the desert that claims them" by Daniel Gonzalez for USA Today details the plight of immigrants attempting to cross the desert that units northern Mexico and southern Arizona. You can read it here: https://www.usatoday.com/border-wall/story/immigration-mexico-border-deaths-organ-pipe-cactus/608910001/.

"The Chickens" refers to Matthew 23:37, the Bible.

"A Tattoo is Inked Over Our Scars" references Gethsemane, the garden in which Jesus, presumably, spent his final hours as a free man praying for his followers as his sweat, according to Luke 22:44, became "drops of blood." [source: the Bible]

"Gomorrah" is a reference to the mythical city portrayed in Genesis 19 of the Bible. According to lore, this city, as well as its sister city Sodom, were destroyed by God, a deity enraged by its violent behavior and material indulgences. Erroneously, this story is often cited to represent the deity's displeasure with homosexuality though the ancient text clearly decries the people's excess and exploitation—a willingness to harm members of a society for personal gain. Sexuality, in general, is not a focus of the text.

Issa's line of poetry in "Poem [with Garden & Ghost & Issa]" is from a haiku on the death his child. The full haiku is "Dew evaporates / and all our world / is dew ... So dear, / So fresh, so fleeting."

"Consider the Loquat" was written as a response to a call for poems for a loquat festival in Florida. Though I never heard back from the festival submission, I did get this beautiful poem out of the exercise, and it was eventually published in *Relief Journal*. The poem's title refers to an often-quoted verse in Matthew 6:28 of the Bible.

Acknowledgements

Thank you to the following journals for publishing separate pieces from this manuscript: *Midwest Quarterly, Slipstream, Natural Bridge, Relief Journal, Moon City Review, riverSedge, Sierra Nevada Review, West Texas Literary Review, Flyover Country, The Meadow, The Idaho Review, Cider Review Press, Mom Egg Review, NELLE, Oyster River Pages, Two Hawks Quarterly, The Comstock Review, West Trade Review, Naugatuck River Review, Great Lakes Review, The 3288 Review, Spirit, The Voices Project, Anti-Heroin Chic, MockingHeart Review, The Raleigh Review, Hashtag Queer: LGBTQ + Creative Anthology*, and *The Lansing Arts Council Journal.*

Special thank you to Dennis Hinrichsen for guiding me in the process of drafting some of these poems and pulling together the manuscript. I am lucky to work with such a wonderful poet and friend.

Additional thanks to Luke Johnson and Rebecca Evans for reviewing and providing feedback on the finished manuscript.

Thank you to Monson Arts in Monson, Maine for providing me with a residency that allowed me to see these poems differently and put the final touches on the manuscript, as well as the opportunity to indulge in the beauty of rural Maine.

For the cover art, I purchased a cigarette case from an Etsy shop in Kyiv City, Ukraine and wish to express my gratitude to the owner of RetroStoreUaByVitaly. Thank you Vitalii. I am so happy to have this beautiful, functional art piece in my possession and to have the opportunity to support someone in this, presently, war torn country.

And I appreciate poet and photographer Justin Hamm's willingness to edit the photo I took of the cigarette case for my cover art. I have a good eye, but my photo editing skills are limited. Lucky to have someone who was willing to collaborate with me on this piece. Thanks Justin!

Mostly importantly, an immense debt of gratitude to my children who have lived these poems with me in real time and again in these words.

Finally, Kory, thank you for the friendship we shared in the early years of our marriage. Our genesis cannot be replicated. I remember.

About the Author

Kimberly Ann Priest is the winner of the 2024 Backwaters Prize in Poetry from the University of Nebraska Press for her book *Wolves in Shells* and the author of *Slaughter the One Bird* (Sundress Publications), finalist for the 2021 American Best Book Awards. Her chapbooks include *The Optimist Shelters in Place* (Harbor Editions), *Parrot Flower* (Glass Poetry Press) and *still life* (PANK) and her work has appeared in *Copper Nickel, Beloit Poetry Journal,* and *The Birmingham Poetry Review* as well as the second edition of *Environmental and Nature Writing: A Writer's Guide and Anthology* from Bloomsbury Academic. She is an assistant professor of first-year writing at Michigan State University and a volunteer teaching artist for young writers at The Telling Room in Portland, Maine.

years later

Not Human

Alma College, Michigan

One of my students says he is a plant: he seeks
categorization because the world's major religions understand him as
not human, he says,

referring to his sexual orientation, which is not like mine,
but those several moments of conversation with my student—his eyes
looped and dancing, his thin pink lips, the pitch and fall of his
jocular tongue—inform me

that I am also a plant: petaled and leafed, folded into the curl of a stalk,
rooted. Less frightening than a moth, more vulnerable than a weed.

Even the rain could crush me.

I wake one morning with my lips bruised by mist and lie there
shaking—half-open, half-broken, half-withered, half-revived—waiting for
the sun to unfurl my limbs, lick steam out of my ears, dry mud
streaming down my thighs until

it crumbles into dust, as the cup of my nectary is siphoned by a stem.
And then,

I bold open—flower flowers, leaves leaf, roots stretch and crawl into
the earth until I'm identified by some passerby who plucks me, takes me
home, and holds me in a vase.